FLOWER GRAND FIRST

FLOWER GRAND FIRST

poems

Gustavo Hernandez

MOON
TIDE PRESS

~ 2021 ~

Flower Grand First
© Copyright 2021 Gustavo Hernandez

Editor-in-chief
Eric Morago

Associate Editor
José Enrique Medina

Editor Emeritus
Michael Miller

Marketing Director
Dania Alkhouli

Marketing Assistant
Ellen Webre

Proofreader
Jim Hoggatt

Front cover art
Gustavo Hernandez

Author photo
Richard Sanchez

Book design
Michael Wada

Moon Tide logo design
Abraham Gomez

Flower Grand First
is published by Moon Tide Press

Moon Tide Press
6709 Washington Ave. #9297, Whittier, CA 90608
www.moontidepress.com

FIRST EDITION

Printed in the United States of America

ISBN # 978-1-7350378-3-7

For Juan Zárate y Guadalupe Hurtado, my parents

CONTENTS

THREE

WRITING INTO BEING: THE POETRY OF GUSTAVO HERNANDEZ

Flower. Grand. First. These are names of streets, but together they mean something more than the names of streets. We come to them with our own connotative meanings. For me, *Flower* is my grandmother. Her cutting and arranging. *Grand* is a piano, a gesture, a velvet hall. It is the Vegas room my grandmother, my sister, and I snuck into that was used in the movie *Indecent Proposal*. *First* is a dance, or perhaps a place in line. And yes, these are also street names in Santa Ana, and yes, this is also where my grandmother lived and where we rented a hot dog cart downtown and passed out hot dogs on Christmas Eve, and where I may have passed Gustavo Hernandez when I was still a child, before I knew him, before I knew his poetry.

And isn't it fortuitous that the first time Gustavo and I met was at an Ada Limón reading, and that we share that magical evening? Ada Limón, the poet that in "What It Looks Like to Us and the Words We Use" writes, "I believe in this connection we all have / to nature, to each other, to the universe," and then "we looked up at the unruly sky, / its clouds in simple animal shapes we could name / though we knew they were really just clouds— / disorderly, and marvelous, and ours.

And then, a year later, we read together in Long Beach, the city of my own childhood. My hometown. Now these words *Flower Grand First* will make me think of this collection of poems, and I am overcome with the capacity of the world to surprise and delight us, and the ability of these poems and this poet to capture what couldn't otherwise be captured. To put down on the page what is "disorderly, and marvelous, and ours."

As individuals, our world is both small and vast. The things that happen to us are infinitely personal and wildly universal. Hernandez has written a book of poems that is up to the challenge of trying to make sense of the paradoxes that are life, memory, family, place, and personality. They use language in a way that expands its scope.

Scholar Gloria Anzaldúa offered this insight into her own need to write: "Why am I compelled to write?... Because the world I create in the writing compensates for what the real world does not give me. By writing I put order in the world, give it a handle so I can grasp it. I write because life does not appease my appetites and anger... To become more intimate with myself and you. To discover myself, to preserve myself, to make myself, to achieve self-autonomy. To dispel the myths that I am a mad prophet or a poor suffering soul."

A book like *Flower Grand First* remakes a writer through language. It is a testament to the innumerable emotions we all experience as humans, but it provides its reader with that handle that Anzaldúa mentions— with a way to tangibly hold the world and its contents. It is a book that not only documents an immigrant experience, but that also sings of the individual's experience. It explores and charts the intersections, the difficulties, and the joys of Hernandez's journey, and in doing so, opens new space for understanding, for empathy, and for connection.

Hernandez's book begins with "California," and takes us between the two spaces of Jalisco, Mexico and Southern California (most notably Santa Ana, but Mission Viejo, Long Beach, and other So. Cal locations also make appearances). In the last lines of the poem, Hernandez writes, "One of my vocabularies / compliantly slips under the other. I want your light / to cross-cut into me and show them that my favorite / thing about this place is that my father brought me here." The importance of place and family figure substantially in this collection, but there is also a sense that luck is always at play, that who we are born to and where we end up are always a matter of providence and its mysterious workings in the world. It is our appreciation of our circumstances, our willingness to embrace our people and places and how they intersect, that allow us to be most fully human.

In "Pecs," Hernandez addresses the theme of luck at a bar in San Diego with his brother, writing,

> Luck is all
> we talk about.
> Our country still down south,
>
> both our parents sleeping
> right up I-5.
> At one a.m. the mirror

in the dark restroom
steadies. Focus.
Look how far you've come,

drunk with three cities
in your mouth...

There is a deep appreciation here for where the speaker is. We, as
readers, are lucky to be there, in the bar, experiencing this moment,
which might make us think of those moments in our own lives where
all seems momentarily right in the world, "The sweet spot / in a
Saturday night / where it opens up and wide..."

Hernandez's poetry collection is not chronological, which gives
the book a suppleness, a stretching across time and place. This is
the superpower that writing gifts an author — an unfolding into
understanding, a growing-into one's place in the world that is
documented in these poems. Take, for example, "Simpson-Mazzoli," a
powerful poem about the 1986 Simpson-Mazzoli Act, which begins,

Little brother is asked to describe our father:
Brown, chubby, in-the-other-room.

The same woman asks me what I did yesterday.
I don't tell her I prayed for chest hair,

for the tail-end of puberty to claim my squat nose,
for blue-green eyes that look good against a tan.

I'll be Héctor Soberón from the novelas—
he speaks Spanish but people think he's handsome.

There is no other Simpson-Mazzoli poem that contains a wish for chest
hair or a mention of Héctor Soberón. It is the honesty and specificity
of this memory that allows the reader to feel both the drift and the heft
of the poem. The changes that are occurring both inside and outside
the narrator, the paradoxical seriousness and lightness of this moment.
This elasticity that memory and language provide can also be seen later,
"with this new body I'm stretching into / with this new body I may
yet receive." Hernandez's poetry fully embraces flux – the flux that is
in our bodies, the flux of the universe, the flux that language offers, its
elasticity, its possibilities.

The fluidity of time and space in Hernandez's poetry sometimes sweeps us into the past. In "1990/20XX" we go between 1990, the "outline of an avocado tree and a television / antenna" (remember those?) but

> The future was
> a McDonald's commercial where the moon
> plays a grand piano in a rented tux.
> The future was the DNA remix
> of *Tom's Diner*. Not this sad finite iridescence.

Hernandez shifts effortlessly between the natural world, the material world, and pop culture. If you haven't heard "Tom's Diner" in a while, take a listen. If you were alive when it came out, it will transport you back to that space and time. Reading this poem while playing the DNA remix of "Tom's Diner" is its own unique joy. A few poems later, the narrator of "Turquoise" wears a Tiger Scout uniform shirt purchased at a garage sale to school, where a teacher tells him, *"You're only supposed to wear that shirt if you are in Tiger Scouts. / Do you know what that is? / You're not supposed to wear that. / Your mother isn't supposed to let you."* Here Hernandez examines what it means to belong... the learning that is necessary, the many ways we adapt to fit in, the many ways we are made to feel as if we don't, the strange rules society is always setting out for us to stumble into.

We get glimpses of how Hernandez came to be a writer, including a lyric, narrative poem, "Juan Lolo" about writing letters for Juan Lolo: "There you marveled / at the speed of the pen and the facility of my composition— / the lexicon of passionate phrases culled from novela / actresses and the lines lifted straight from Jane Austen / novels..." Hernandez is both Jalisco and Santa Ana, he is inspired by novella actresses and Jane Austen, he is an amalgamation of all of these, a flourishing, or as it is put in "How to Be a Heartbreaker," "A working body prying the slick door / open between dimensions."

The narrative poems work both as stories and metaphors, while simultaneously moving us into a future place. In "Sunday, San Gabriel Valley," Hernandez writes, "A week after I kissed him just because I could, / he nearly brought me into the house / to meet his dying mother. / Instead, he delivered the flowers, / and I was left in the car rolling / the peeled-off barcode between my fingers." Here are the narrative happenings that are what they are, but which are also things that morph and shift into other possibilities for meaning. The speaker takes action because he can, a man's mother is dying, a label is peeled away. Life is shifting before our eyes — someone of a past generation leaving, a companion's life is reflected in the "peeling yellow of a restaurant," and "crumbling parking stops" and then the poem suddenly opens out: "forty miles south, / without the need for me to think of it, / my family was a doorway / expanding, whole, all tomorrows."

There is always a mystery to these poems, a layering, a new dimension opening. Hernandez has a gift for both telling the truth but also, as Emily Dickinson has written, telling it "slant." In this type of telling, the truth expands to hold more than just the facts. There is a longing in these poems, a longing for place and sound, for the natural world and the man-made, for people and touch and history. In "Santa Ana: First Street," Hernandez captures the train whistle without ever describing its actual sound. Instead it is "a sugar. Let me not reduce it / to its cargo, let me not reduce it / to box cars, to boxes. I want / to keep it a song whose words / come from the still-glowing signs / of the bakeries and the swap malls, / of the buildings that once fed us & / once clothed us & maybe once / let us dance inside them."

The book suggests the growth, or a reckoning with life, of a man who has come into his own. A kind of poetry bildungsroman, where the protagonist has circled back to where he had originated, but transformed. And we, as readers, are also transformed; we are in "Noviembre," arriving to the United States' "day-old Halloween candy," arriving to a life, "*So my kids can work in an office with air conditioning*," or arriving in "Santa Ana: Downtown," with its wild parrots and the "laughter / of men who could make even coffee / bloom." We are there for the "Otay Crossing" and at the "Aliso Creek Rest Stop, I-5-SB," so that when we end up at the last poem, "The Hereafter," we see the stunning outcome of writing oneself into existence, the culmination of these words leading us back to a moment where it "will always be Jalisco."

Welcome to *Flower Grand First*, where this is all just beginning, with luck, with a title, with an incredibly talented poet, with a table of contents and an epigraph, and language that has been shaped into universes. And when you arrive at the end of this book, which is its own beginning, suddenly the epigraph from Agustin Yáñez, who was a writer and the governor of Jalisco from 1953-1959, will read as if it has always been meant for Hernandez's magnificent collection of poems. As readers, we too come full circle, but with a new understanding of what an abundant life really means, in all of its complexities, and with a new understanding of the myriad ways poetry can touch and expand our hearts.

— Alexandra Umlas

We'll never find what we're looking for in distant places, and the very thought of abandoning the land is wrong unless it's to bring back to the land what it needs.

— Agustín Yáñez

ONE

CALIFORNIA

What else could anyone make
    of your new constellation: white
        rubber soles burning with a tight white
                            glow
            beneath the void-void black
            of some new Nikes.

Check the cut of the shorts,
          the too-high hem.
          You can trace its shape
     down the coast, there
              is not a pure Mexican drop of sky
              inside it.

I am walking down a sidewalk on E. Ocean
         washed in this and other lights.
    To someone like me, even the coast
        should be foreign.

Moon horns
          open to the south. One of my vocabularies
          compliantly hides under the other.

I want your light to cross-cut into me
              to show them
    that my favorite thing about this place
        is that my father brought me here.

REFUGIO

In the early morning there's a sweetness
in the white smoke rising from our houses.
It is December and the night mist has left
behind its small complications. They are
water on dry corn stalks. It is everywhere:
rooster feather, tractor wheel, the largest
nativity scene en el rancho, where even
the devil is gold-flaked. This is and isn't
memory, because I am trying to tell you
of a time when only my grandmother
was left to walk across our patio.
Years after she stomped across it
to undo the rusty deadbolt to the room
my sister had locked me in. Years after
she guided my hands across it to wash up
in my mom's lavadero. After we were all
gone. Living in El Norte. No, y yo pa que
voy? Y quien va a echarle agua a la salia?
O al arrayán? O a las rosas y a los aretes?
I am filling in words now, too. See, I am
trying to make sense of it for you, for us,
because on this side, things grow
on their own whether someone goes or stays.
I'm trying to make this okay for you. Show
you I can still feel her missing me, in this
body: no shirt in a stainless-steel kitchen,
hairy chest and the crow's feet, my glasses.
I am trying to show you there's never a day
when the hills don't unfold in light and dew
and smoke.

SIMPSON-MAZZOLI

In 1986 the Simpson-Mazzoli Act made it illegal to knowingly hire undocumented immigrants, but also paved the way to citizenship for some immigrants and their families.

Little brother is asked to describe our father:
Brown, chubby, in-the-other-room.

The same woman asks me what I did yesterday.
I don't tell her I prayed for chest hair,

for the tail-end of puberty to claim my squat nose,
for blue-green eyes that look good against a tan.

I'd be Héctor Soberón from the novelas—
he speaks Spanish, but he's handsome.

I don't tell her about the doctor's exam
that touched and counted me

suddenly, two by two—
round and red-faced—two by two.

    I don't tell her about the Tijuana dog races
    across the street from our motel room,

        the Magic Fingers coin acceptor
        that my mother covered up with her sweater,

            the pulsing of the alcohol and bodies
            all around us that I couldn't see but sensed

                with this new body I'm stretching into
        with this new body I may yet receive.

My older sister reins us in, hides us
in her speech, makes us look presentable.

The wood-paneled office wavers, hollow to gravid
as the immigration agent mulls it over.

She trims a waning bloom from her desk bouquet.
Her fingernails make the whole world tick—

a burgundy lacquer, a clip and a click.

LUPITA

Sister. We have
    joined a country in mid step
    the dried milk in the fridge
    we've inherited makes
    a smell strange and thick

Remember. August rain
    making new paths for our feet
    our father's sweet call
    to all the young
    stalks of the earth

Listen. Downtown
    the city buses settle themselves
    under the yellow mist of streetlights
    entire blocks wind down in the quick fire
    of recycled late-night monologues

On the outskirts. The yards
    are already full of old wrecks
    crumpled concepts
    outmoded novelty
    decades of scrap

SANTA ANA, FOURTH GRADE

Is that the fairy? Our voices
all squeak, so this question isn't
about that. Someone's been paying
attention and again I am named
before I have understood myself.
Someone has discovered me—
a girl who is the cousin of a boy
I thought and called my friend.
A boy who's named himself
white trash because he is among us.
Someone has discovered me
chaining the clovered horizon to garland.
They've seen the crushed jacaranda
paste on my palms. So, this
is the spot where I branch out in purple.
Here, where the popsicle melts its red
and its blue, this one street, wide
as a landing strip, heat waves rippling
into invisible, asphalt markings that lead
up to them like a parable to temptation.

THE DIRK YATES GUIDE TO NATURALIZATION

The man behind the camera says all
it takes is a few beers and a hundred
bucks. My mind slips between the layers
of tan tweed, between two Marines
and their white hotel sheets.

The news footage is only bare backs
and the foaming throat of Oceanside,
a lamp of blue eyes. I guess

who is the border. What is the passport.

Imagine the yellow stucco balcony
showing me the whole Pacific
beneath a belt unlatching,
that rent in this country's expensive.

And I want it,
the end of this illegal body,
to run around here, there, fully fourteen
and growing to the end of this gelatin stasis.

The news footage is a shot of a bicep,
the exhausted girth
of cotton towels, the sergeant
saying that his men will not be punished
because they're part of the structure.

It'll blow over.

And I want it.
A promise that I can swell
in that same light, that my wet neck

will also be pushed down into dark silver
archives. That what I spill, what I record,
what is congealed will also be forgotten

because no one will be looking for it.

1990/20XX

Some nights I'd sit in any open driveway space.
Across the street the skyline was a dim bulb
outline of an avocado tree and a television
antenna. Beyond, the future was
a searchlight. One of those Hollywood premier
numbers. The future was
a McDonald's commercial where the moon
plays a grand piano in a rented tux.
The future was the DNA remix
of "Tom's Diner." Not this sad finite iridescence.

How a truck can go from orange cream
to scarab shell to that loud sweetness
he called burgundy then disappear
even though its downshifting
always sounded so long-breath hopeful.

All night the city holds its color
still to signal what is missing.
The eastern stretch of First Street
won't unclasp into the hills. Not one grain
of earth decides
to release another. The spray paint messages
dry and sink into the murals:
The night used to ring out in synthesizer bells.
Here is where they sat and counted one another.
You see, there had been a father.

SUMMER BURLAP BUNDLE '98

Mustard grass. Rose and sago trimmings for an extra twenty. Mustard grass. The county inspector's mustache hair and drops of melted sunblock. Mustard grass. Lizard scurrying down a driveway. Rattlesnake eggs. Gasoline mixed with engine oil. An accusation hurled by a homeowner's son drunk at noon. Mustard grass and rattlesnake eggs. The groan of weed-wackers over the hills. Over millions of old dollars. Mustard grass. Freeway traffic and bad jokes on the AM radio. Mustard grass. Our old gate rolling open. A whistling at the doorway.

FLECHA AMARILLA

My dad liked to tell
a story about how I
once ended up on
the floor mat of his truck for
looking over the dashboard

I liked to call out
all the Jalisco bus lines—
the riders and their
public pilgrimages, roads
stretched to noon to night to roads

In a new country
he'd teach me to watch my speed,
to only drive when
necessary, the danger
of blind spots, of eagerness

I liked the landscape
and its crisscross brush of green
that slowly warmed once
all the horses had begun
to graze and the night hawks slept

7 LEGUAS

After the bartender makes up some fake
Tuesday three-for-one special, my brother
does an impression of my uncle—it's perfect.
How his throat goes sharp and ragged, how
he gets the quick cadence and the indispensable
joke-propelling stutter. We are knocking around
lost somewhere in our twenties. Missing
and making so much. In this moment there is honesty
and, of course, it is understood and unspoken. We
lift the summer dust, separate it from the concrete
with our new shoes, our dropped baseball caps
and open a stream through time—past, distance,
(somehow) future. For a moment we completely
join him and my father, our elders and ancestors,
who are beleaguered compatriots, waylaid jokesters.
The impression of my uncle—his charm—is respect,
admiration. It will be hard to get it right again.

LATE NIGHT FORMULA 44 COMMERCIAL

When he's told his child is ill,
the shepherd drives through
a field of electric lanterns.
He puts a purple plastic bottle
in his wife's hands, asks her
to remember the number—the word
formula is the same, recognizable
as a sprig of rue, an oregano leaf.

TURQUOISE

Tell your mom you can't wear that shirt anymore,
says the teacher on monitor duty.
His arm sprouting goldenrod.
It motions to my turquoise Tiger Scouts shirt.

Turquoise is my favorite color.
He knows I'm not a Tiger Scout.
Tell your mom not to let you wear that shirt anymore.

1987
I own one new shirt—
a souvenir from my Tía Rosario's trip to Vegas,
white and printed with teddy bears
huddled around a pool table.

The others are paid for with quarters and dimes
at garage sales
in middle-class neighborhoods,
Spanish street names that don't make sense.
I brush my teeth twice.
I find my best shoes to go there.

You're only supposed to wear that shirt if you are in Tiger Scouts.
Do you know what that is?
You're not supposed to wear that.
Your mother isn't supposed to let you.
My son is a Tiger Scout.
You're not supposed to buy that shirt for a quarter at a yard sale.

The shirt is hidden in the sewing closet.
Tiger eyes peek over pastoral cross-stitch scenes.
Tiger claws caught on crochet loops.

When it's time to go shopping again
I look for more shirts with wild animals.
I do it for the goldenrod arm.
I do it hoping to trick my mother,
so she won't ask about the missing
turquoise flash in the laundry pile.

I look for more
but I'm careful.
    Safari '79
    Circus '83

The recess monitor checks on me daily,
    to make sure.

    Safari '79
    Circus '83

He knows what we should
and shouldn't do.

But he doesn't know
who truly gets to pick
a t-shirt.

VEINTITRÉS

Two men have brought one set of parents
to this dark wood Long Beach bar
where, with the door open, the heat glimmer
makes the alcohol hover like vapor
just above the skin as if outside the blood.
The mother dances to a pulsing beat, yells
across the bar in a Wisconsin accent,
and I cross out words in an article
about genetics, an article about expecting
a sure thing from the white of your body
and receiving a piece of land you've already
lived in. Pop science in a free magazine
with tight swim trunks on the cover, one
where the brown abs were always formerly
pink. Always formerly something else.
The strikethroughs show me disappointment
in the percentages, hidden in the other words,
and this isn't new. Dark settling or evaporating.
That's how we know we are all still trying
for someone else. Why we feel reduced
by the red hair not meaning what we thought
it meant. After a drink, the woman pulls her son
(or his partner) to the dance floor; she takes
his hand, brings out all of her
old disco moves, and I wonder how
it feels to move low-coiled, circling, electric,
to never guess where you came from, to not
have it make a difference, to see time moving
solid in front of you, thinking it complete.

CARMEN

The four walls of the Setco Plastics Factory
were built around my sister's name—its red
lip, its pride, its dark hair pulled up to where
she couldn't see it. Her words were sifted
through a wall of exhaust fans, lost
as the second shift pushed the city
to the edges of a new cycle. The light again
drained from Flower, from Grand, from First.

On most nights, she and I met
in the artificial glow of our television—
belts of stars soaked into the gold leg
scrolls of telenovela chairs. I was
kept awake by chaining meaning
to other manufactured sounds—fat
syllables of my name maneuvering through
the blades of lean foreign words.

There was one night in July, where a mute girl
in the novela willed the words back to her mouth
to tell Arturo Peniche that his fiancé
had been a terrible villain. I told you
she'd get her voice back. Carmen's tone
was tempered flat through repetition. Bottles
and bottles and plastic cereal containers
evenly spaced on a conveyor belt.

She motioned for me to join her
at the open front door. From the street, she was
fading red lipstick; I was an electric blue
garage sale t-shirt. The moon played
with the overgrown ficus. June bugs spun
around a porch light, but we looked past them
and dreamt a far-off language.

FORMAS SAGRADAS

To a child, the Virgenes return mechanized
over the pitayas in the countryside. Night masses
of steel braids and copper manteaus over Atotonilco
and its ruby wealth, breathing dahlia blossoms
from the vents in their joints, magnetized segments
hovering warm sighs away from each other. Circles

of stars around their fingers raised in benediction,
these ticking-brass mothers leak milk, bake bread
keep watch over and irrigate the guasana fields.
Bone white face panels shift—crescent, bullhorn
new to full—to illuminate the way for children
herding cattle. How these whirring monoliths

return us to the old way—synthesized blessings
over the hands of old men offering papayas
and mangos de los de antes. To a child, these
mothers are the black mist of manufactured
thunderclouds purifying veins, disarming men.
Healers of the grief of widows and the childless.

How their knees slowly trail down the illuminated
walkways of their templos. Paying back mandas:
the sick injected to health, the work remunerated,
the land kept. Crying children convince their
reluctant parents to enter, to not ever feel afraid.
These mothers are the same as ever. Call to them.

JUAN LOLO

On Saturdays, in my parents' garage
I wrote letters in your name. You sat back against
the utility shelves that housed your one silk shirt
and your six-days-worth of work clothes. I sat
at the edge of the bed, steno pad on my lap,
facing the garage door and the nights crowded
with cumbia melodies. You marveled
at the speed of the pen and the facility of my composition—
the lexicon of passionate phrases culled from novela
actresses and the lines lifted straight from Jane Austen
novels that I roughly translated for a woman
almost 2000 miles south. I was newly distanced
from childhood, barely beyond a sophomore growth spurt.
And these letters. The only letters I'd ever write
that would open with "Querida." It was your job
to fill in numbers: the date of your next visit,
how much of your landscaping check could be put away
each month to help her cross into this country.
And sometimes we'd take a break to look
at the formation of the stars, to hear the night move
with the clicking of high heels on the concrete sidewalks.
You'd brush your teeth in the dark; you'd spit
into the planters. And before the air mail envelope
was sealed I'd read to you her last reply: she
couldn't wait to see you. She said she loved you too.
And it was a response to my words, my crooked
handwriting, my rhyme and my well-wishes for you.

BAUDELIA

Grand mal seizures. My guess it was
my Tía Baudelia's burden, all
of these decades later, from what
my mother tells me. All of her life

in Jalisco, at the foot of a plateau, some
wilderness, in the disadvantage of an era,
to us, now, the disadvantage of old time,
in an adobe house, in the mist. El gran mal.

When my grandmother died, her daughters
thought they saw the source of her cancer
take the shape of an owl and fly into
the dry, moonlit ruffle of a guamúchil.

In town, depressed women were explained
by poison fed to them in food flavored
with envy or by the hands of jilted lovers.
But Baudelia was different—what ill will

could befall someone who lived clutching
her mother's rebozo her entire life? A sickness.
A sadness. Poor child. Poor girl. Poor woman.
I guess at her half-living in a stasis. I paint joy

in the warm dirt patios of spring, ear to a rustle
and glint of a finch song in the nochebuena,
the warmth of the stone oven in her parents'
kitchen, the blossoms of her sisters' fortunes.

My mother says when I was born, she asked
to hold me. That I felt her arms outstretching.
Her breath expanding.
Give him to me, Lupe.
I can hold him. I won't drop him. I won't get sick.

DOMINGO, SAN ISIDRO, JAL.

After church, the banda plays
for teenage boys
living up to their fathers.

They are swept into dark corners,
learning and feeling, early,
    exactly as it is written.

With what they think to be secret
marks and secret knowledge,
they emerge before their shawled mothers

who are laughing and sighing
spearmint gum and violet perfume
    and futures and good matches—
    no bad blood between the families.

And I am around town too,

shooed from my mother's side,
scattered, stopping, looking
for a way back. Expectantly

watched—in her boasting
I am always just a memory
of a large golden child.

SANTA ANA, 1995

I may have been surrounded by the city's losses—
maybe a morning drawn in dead carburetors
or the sad hung-over math of early July—

but all around our fathers had become
small proprietors. Sixteen, and the hills
and roads of America were said to be disorganized
only because they were, on the whole, open.

At the bus stop in plaid cotton shorts
and a Tori Amos t-shirt, palming
a high school collage of black
and white Versace ads, hungry

and buoyant, I was a probable answer.
I'd been trained to stare holes into the future.

SANTA ANA AT SIXTEEN

Play side A again

> me, from under
> the sunset
> shadowgraphs
> of an orange tree

North there is a street called Myrtle

> where among the arms
> of lovers and the hopeful
> cries of vendors
> mostly crab grass
> and begonias grow

But fast-forward to song two

> my sister flips
> her bootleg Shakira tape,
> pushes the boombox
> against the screen
> of the window,
> gets back to her addition
> and subtraction

There's a field just south of Willits

> where another
> boy's at practice,
> running laps,
> unknowingly
> absorbing sound

Flip the tape over again.

And the sparrows and the neighbors and my parents

can't quite seem
to ask me why. They're
not ready. I'm not ready,

but the DJ knows what's up.

TWO

HOW TO BE A HEARTBREAKER

I am a slow, slow boy and the ceiling
of the room descends, bass-beating,
measuring these men—
their GRAYSKULL heft, measuring
only the belt and the muscle.
Picture them evenly matched, evenly
skilled, even-steven, block-jawed hard.
Imagine them always knowing where
the hot blast will hit before the sword
is even drawn—a God's aim across
the room. And through this summer
I've been pulling myself apart, melting
what is left with my version of their fire.
The man who knows all of their drinks
asks why he's never seen me here before,
but the echo of my arm pushing a twenty
toward him travels back, finding
its approximate shape for weeks. I am
changing, re-forming to visibility. This
is discipline: flexing as greeting.
These are men. God's aim. Me, soon.
A new body prying the slick door
open between dimensions, filling
a black ceiling with a prayer-smoke image,
an inversion. Imagine above you
a fat-cheeked boy, his belly keeping him
there eternally, watching.

PUNTO DE CRUZ

Under the red bougainvillea canopy
he was blessed with faultless vines
and blooming yellow floribunda roses.
Needles and primary colors warming
through the clearings opened up to
the Jalisco sun. He came with his mother.
My mother says his work was better
than theirs. He was alone. Distinguished.
A good companion. Saturdays: pressing
two outfits for eight a.m. mass. Mornings:
warming the cinnamon tea for his mother.

There was another she knew, and he paid
a man for his eyes, his hands, for the grip
that the shovel and rake didn't drain.
Summers through a screen door and plain-
wrap beer in California, the steam of his pores
made the money he sent past the solid-line
border grow lighter. My mother saw his wife's
hungry mouth zip tight with subtraction.

When you left, on the evening she met you
and cried, I asked her if those were the only
two ways she saw me in love—birthright
or bartering—and the direction that she'd
pushed me in not teaching me to cross-stitch.

HURTADO

At twenty-five,
though there is no Quarter Horse,
my body, too, has come
together, but in a poured road
split of scrub oak
and pineapple weed

Feel your blood
against the law, among the modern
and mechanical, without
a doubt, thinking it owns
and can corral and tame
and brand another

In a canyon
I've had midnight easily spoken
to me in falling coral vine,
whispered praise dripping
through white-coated
adobe and flat brick
work

And my chest,
another dark field flowering,
another sturdy mesa rising,
balancing the August heat,
a feeling, like an arm
around an old rope trick.

HOOKUP #1

I drove the eleven miles to your house
and on the way no longer bothered
the chaparral or the mountain
with questions. I couldn't imagine spring
as a wife. In your living room
it was a small, framed reproduction
of the Newport Coast, light and easy,
a maze of veined marble tile under my feet.
Leading with the light head of a wounded
man—more than that three days' worth—
I wanted to say I'd saved everything
for you: the warmth of my truck
to the things that had buckled
and curved in my memory, like you
have now. And I don't mind
that your name was lost to the demand
of summer. I still see the warming planter,
the bachelor's button fully grown, and there
we are, unlimbering the biggest thing
we thought we could offer each other.

ZAK SPEARS BARTENDS AT THE FAULTLINE (C. 2002)

for Rudy

We walk in half-hexed by sun,
the light inside a softer appraiser.
The whole place is wet with summer
answers. It is two in the afternoon.

And everyone is low light, going
from sermon to hymn, semaphore
to boxing drill. We are low light—
all haunches and confidence.

Let's call each other grown among
bodies that say nothing else. Muscle
mature, bristling curved, capable
capable. Let's call each other grown

in the center of the city, crushed
out and ecstatic, flanked by what
we say we want. But say you still hear
our parents calling into our rooms,

our nieces as children; say you can
still feel the chain-link fences,
the gardenias growing through them.
It is early enough.

FORMAS MODERNAS

Tonight, my mother's prayers are registered high
somewhere above date palms and freeway signs.

And below that white-lacquered satellite, I am
heedless, just bathed and insolent. New amplified

litanies vibrate through the walls, hold me
in their low glittering, drenched and heavy

in fuzz and gold distortion. I'm prayed over
by mothers in studs & cardinal lipstick, Our Lady

of the DC 59, of the Fender Twin, of the Hot Pink
Wash of Spring Reverb. Modern like a photon ray

the message burns but remains what it has always been:
All your friends in LA don't love you like I love you.

A BAD BIRTHDAY DEDICATION

A sorry apology blueprint.
This time for being late
to a party. This time for
the piece of road debris
that hit the bumper going 90
away from a freckled man
who asked if I ever thought
I'd get to be with a muscle-
head like him. His generosity.

Repeating apology blueprint.
My mom will see my body
and will recognize it as a
temporal echo—the cycle
of excuses of a man who is dead.
His numbers and his secrets.
A blade separating two colors
before they melt into each other.
The girth of an orange grove
that vanishes as it cools.

I will take the water bottle
my brother hands me; sit next to
my father, a mirror of his faithful
temperance. Quote a verse
from a rap song for my sister.
Make her laugh through the gloss
of her red lipstick. Sixteen bars
pulling the night in, catching
pieces of the truth in brag.

Red, I'll make myself a clown
for my young nieces, pop a balloon
and suddenly fall to the ground,
my body weighed down
by the afternoon, by the leaves
in the plastic pool, by the even
weight of hope and disappointment.

HEART LIKE A WHEEL

It is true some of us left old lovers
to bad marriages, old boyfriends
to die in automobile crashes
maneuvering some famous unlit
curve made perfect by the rains
of July, by the golden yellow
of a Mexican pilsner that was
by then glowing only on the inside.

It is cruel that the letters should stop
crossing, that we should be cut off
even from a retelling of how
our pueblos continue to move
independently of us. Here we count
the hours until the sun comes up
and it's always the same stale
number that places us between

getting up for the graveyard
shift and the chicken place
down the street closing. We
can recall evening lukewarm
showers, perfume on the walks
around the plaza, but only see
sidewalks stretched
made to look like a horizon.

Motion. We're all sick with it,
from the night we are brought
here, primed to fall for this
country's first volley of electric
arrows. A blur from a back seat
that reduces love to a narrowing
need for something to let you
keep moving within it.

TUBEROSE

Illumination, camino de la noche,
      my father and his childhood
                friend reached out for you.
Their hands brought light
    down from the foothills.
           Linterna de el brazo moreno,

the Aztec named you Omixochitl—bone flower

but think of the ease
with which the precision
of a native tongue is dulled, misheard
to take away its fragrant corners

Omixochitl—twin flower
    The perfumed pearl-gemini
            bubbling through each bract

How the poor
are always sent in twos
to procure beauty

      for the good of the town
      for the wealth of our patron
          saints

I think of those boys,
outside the church doors,
a peso in each of their pockets,
their eyes fixed on their accomplishment
    at the foot of the altar,
    on the spume at the foot of faith,

      naming it over
          and over.

MORNING GLORY

The effort of this storm would be called,
all across the towns
of Jalisco, unmatched,
miraculous. But for a time
there was only its insincere
and staged request
for permission: slippery gray
and mist. In this,
she rushed to bring the cows home.
A quick step
up the stone-paved incline
to the ruche of meadow
gathered along the river.
Holding out for her a little longer
were the morning glories, tiny
open lamps of purple and blue
run through rock and custard apple tree.
Across from me in her kitchen
my mother has said many times
that she now feels motionless, that we
seem to do nothing
but move independent of her.
Today she tells a story
about how she cared most
for a calf who was blind in one eye.
The most difficult one, angry
and scared by a dark hemisphere.
She tells about a storm and her voice
calling out, coalescing
into a roll call: Moneda.
Magalona. Mariposa. She says
the cattle obediently responded
to their names, headed south
on a muddying path, ambled
toward her like children.

FLOR DE ALBACAR I

With her hands in the mint and rue
she recalls a large basil bush in Jalisco,
a gift from a compadre, one of many
fathers whose children were carried
to the baptismal pool in my parents' arms
Oh, wealth isn't always money.
We were well-liked. So many godchildren.
Scattered now. Think of a stem growing
north and a bloom spreading: Chicago,
Tejas, Arizona, California. How many
of them called when he died. She goes
through the list.

A WHITE BOY APOLOGY

I don't know what's going on at home,
but February and rain
pool on the lawn of every county
school miles around,
pricked and stirred gray. I am
a weak glint carried
through these valleys, snow
on the tip of the San Gabriels,
another one of California's half-
mouthed phrases, a boy hanging out
with girls born in the foxglove
of only one landscape. They all say
origins don't have to matter.
That now there is one
set of roads. I don't know
what's going on at home. Where
you are, mother and father. Noon
and dusk are indistinguishable. I
don't know which pink or purple bell
will spring from the ground
in a month. If the songbirds are gone
or if they're nesting.

BODY

this is how I worship you—

        by looking down from my face
                in his mirror.

THIRD SHIFT

I told a gas station attendant that I loved you.
It was 2 a.m. You were still at work
and the roadside blooms blew their scent
to me. Staggered, blinking, the stars
were all harp strings plucked on navy
and black—notes descending, dissolving,
shy and disappearing over the coronet
of our mountains. By this time, my courage
had been spent in a ribbon-white rush.
In a hotel room whose backcloth
was the steady voice of a late night talk show
host. Spent on the salt and fur of a stranger's
chest. And only then did I long for home,
for the muted tick of our kitchen clock. Only
then was your factory work heavy upon me,
the blonde and the gray of your roughening face.

WHAT I CAN TELL YOU NOW

In the first slick and blurry sheet of memory
the narrow streets of his neighborhood
are waterways. The banks are birds of paradise
growing tight between parked cars. I peel
for you the night air swollen shut, and it is
cooling weeds and jasmine—open pores.
I can tell you now that he was one of the men
who set me jogging, who kept me hungry.
The one who asked if I felt better, tying
the laces of my Nikes against the archway
of his living room. He'd been
through it, he was right to ask. And I did,
because I was free to return home
to our tiny kitchen, to have a glass of water,
to attend to the mewing of the cats.
You were free to have your last menthol
in the gray of the morning, grab your lunchbox
and come home. And now I can tell you
about a threesome with him some time before:
a room congealed in yellow light—how I wasn't
into the other guy and it made them both
seem unattractive. They smoked a glass pipe
and I declined it, and that, I'm sure, made my
big body seem like the one of an overgrown
child. Their four eyes together tried to harmonize
what we'd already done, and the hair on me,
and how I wouldn't go all the way, with them.

AMERICAN THIGHS

On the first 80° day of the year
it's easy to believe this county
when it sells its borders as soft
or invisible—

to believe myself a part of the road,
the sequence of sunlight. It's my arm
hanging out of the single-cab,
my voice atop the humbucker,

pumping like a homegrown
machine, all overlaid
engineering, daring its men
to find and touch an uninspired angle.

MISA DE GALLO

In late December the nights lack some of their permissiveness.

In the wet decorated hedges, the rich dens
of this neighborhood—maybe in their stillness—
there is something disapproving.

Drained and damp under this cashmere, I think: I've given
    too much to never cross
your line of hydrangea, to still feel
  like a disruption, for these boots

    to make so much noise they give away
my movement
        at this hour, for this to end
                in a concession:

Yes, black dome vault of clouds,
    somewhere I began to trust
my body, my tongue and its brutish but deft curiosity.

No, silent American town,
    I shouldn't be walking here alone.
I shouldn't have done that.
    The couple I deep kissed were only out for a martini
before bed.

ALONG THE 15 NEAR BAKER

a radio signal travels down a small hill,
carried on the winking quartz and granite.
It plays a repeating segment about the Mojave:
cinder cones, rattlers, the importance of cool water.
     The steady voice. The reminder to be careful.

I remind myself of this drive with someone else.
He put his left hand on my knee and wondered aloud
if a Joshua tree could survive in our backyard
     so far south—one more thing we might try to keep alive.

Just like you and I, we didn't stop for the sand in the Mojave.
Just like us, we didn't need to talk so much.
I mention these small things to you, but you're sleeping,
     warm under your own weight, breathing out your own significance.

SUNDAY, SAN GABRIEL VALLEY

A week after I kissed him just because I could,
he nearly brought me into the house
to meet his dying mother.
Instead, he delivered the flowers,
and I was left in the car rolling
the peeled-off barcode between my fingers.
His city was gravel
quarries, some speedway, a dam
taking in the last of the day's red gradient,
and next was the peeling yellow of a restaurant
where the owner knew his father.
On the way there, his childhood was nicked
and pulled through apartment windows
and middle school chain link. With urgency.
The crumbling parking stops. Fingers
pushing between mine, shadow cylinders
of the old brewery disappearing into
the highway. And forty miles south,
without the need for me to think of it,
my family was a doorway
expanding, whole, all tomorrows.

THREE

THE CALL

It all starts with someone's word,
with a church bell echoing in the
foothills, pushing forward the coal-
strong trains, vibrating the hacienda
walls and tornado-turned stone—
a brass eye dissolving in the black-
gemmed river. Someone's word,
a ringing church bell ladling star
and glimmering over scattered
houses, milk skin floating above
corn and kitchen ash. Petroleum
light three hours before dawn. And
the old bones, palms down in cotton
blankets, recognize the burgundy
perimeter the devil pads and hooves
around the churchyard—plated
with the new north, salient
with usury. His old thirst for sons,
his wet border moss sprinkling
and patting down dirt for the young,
for the innocent footfall of morning.

BLAS
for my father

You wanted me to write
about your childhood cat,
back when I still wrote stories.
His size, the strength of the golden
bolt that seized your aunt's dove
as it escaped from its cage—
it was lost to her, anyway.
The way your mother stood there
crying with you
but didn't untie him. Justice
is unstoppable. Your aunt's blood-
for-blood. Her frustration
when the old rope snapped. His strength,
the ascension of dust into the huizaches.

SANTIAGO CANYON

One summer your granddaughter said I'd never grow old
because I still wore shorts and my socks up to mid-calf

but I was thirty-eight, in summer school up on a hill
you tended to before you got sick, before all we didn't make

in this country began to turn on us.
On the way there, I distracted myself with the star thistle,

the odd poppy, the lots I remembered you cleared. In
class I befriended two young girls, and they were kind

enough to see me out. I mentioned them once at your
table, told you their stories, their pressures.

But I want to explain this to you again, Apá. How I blurred
my vision and imagined those slopes were our country's

agave fields, slopes and slopes of that crocodile lotus.
How I hadn't gotten old. How those beautiful girls

quietly walked out of class, mats under their arms
and how the mats rolled out in the orange and sage pressed

into the air, summer, the last one with you. How I felt
their prayers mantle every one of your promises to me;

bless each of the steps you took here; cloak
and float the things I had left, that I'd been fortunate

enough to keep for this long, into the sky. How it was
a ceremony. How their arms held me when it was over.

When you were gone, when I came back to them
full of acknowledgement and oaken with age.

MARTE

Around the time
    the first holiday billboards
        go up

    I raise a finger to a point in the night.

To my eldest sister say,
    look   that red light is Mars.

We have been more than one year
    without him, and just now
        we are starting to see things again.

    So much of our knowledge
about the skies is gone.
        Chart-blind,
            codices black—all questions
    we have forgotten to ask:
            the color of the orbs
            the slabs of moonlight.

I tell her the planet has been
    floating there for weeks,
and I really mean to say,
    we must try to hold on
        to everything we can still recognize,
            even the need to look
    for our fathers
in the
                sky.

FLOR DE ALBACAR II

With her hands in the mint and rue,
she recalls a large basil bush in Jalisco
and tells me she's never had much luck
with it here. It's supposed to be good
luck, and it never seems to take. Next
to the roses, among the snapdragons,

planted with gardenia or sown
with impatiens. Away from the planters
my father built her, I pull money
from my pocket, leave a tie and jacket
in the car, buy and throw five packets
of seed into a small glazed pot
of dark soil I also paid for, to show her
what this place has taught me about luck.

MY FATHER SHOWS ME CATALINA

His footsteps hollow
on someone's deck, a house pushing
off a hill on two wooden beams—
the near impossibility, the foolishness,
and beyond and below,
the green that to him spoke
only of the brown behind it.

He put his hand out descending a slope
to measure out 100 feet, defensible
space. This whole place is seen
as measurements and fire breaks
and noxious native vegetation. A keep-
away, protector. Our homes on this hill
must be kept safe. We'll write you
a check for eighty so they can keep
their seven digits together, worker.

You follow their orders. Stop the machine
if they say it's too early, if they need to
sleep. 100 feet to keep them happy. Smile
so you both know it's okay that you are
different. But once-in-a-while, the division
is so clean it'll cut into you. The division:

clear the wild oat, the sagebrush. Brush
away the eucalyptus. At noon, rest
your back against it, buy grocery store
fried chicken and bread for yourself. Smile
at the cars that leave their driveways, sun-
glasses on blond. Get up. Clear the summer
mustard, free of any kind of hunger.

He says, see how my hand goes, past your mother
in her garden, to the coast, past a place
someone named San Juan, after our own.
All along, there is work, removal and rebirth.
All along the trees and grass will never stop
providing just enough for the hands behind them.

SANTA ANA: FIRST STREET

Because I think you must miss
the dark morning train whistle
through our almost empty streets,
above our houses, its intonation
becomes smoother, maybe even
a sugar. Let me not reduce it
to its cargo, let me not reduce it
to box cars, to boxes. I want
to keep it a song whose words
come from the still-glowing signs
of the bakeries and the swap malls,
of the buildings that once fed us &
once clothed us & maybe once
let us dance inside them.

IMMIGRANT'S NOCTURNE, 1985

My mother hates standard time
even though in both of my hometowns
winter is a black sapphire manicure.
Even though the wave of frost
descends here like it does in San Isidro,
like a sister fakes a threat of violence—

Okay, now pull the claws back.

My mother hates standard time because
it reminds her of the first dark days
shut in these rowed lanterns, uncertain
if the lights' howl and shine meant
safety or injury, safety or separation.

A preparation, a checking, a locking,

a rushing my brother in from his burying
action figures in the front yard, his piggy-
back rides from the men who deal next
door. An hour, a whole hour, in this place
that had already dimmed and taken so much.

The dark fell and looped through months,

but she never thought the cycle would
be permanent. Eventually this whole
place—the dark, the rules, the walls—
would fall away, ringing like a loose-bell
milk tooth. And for her and for us

I wish she'd thought you were magnificent

in those first few weeks, when
grieving meant only doing, only
sorting out the second-hand, only
cleaning, waiting for my father
to come home and speak the light,
the promise that we're going back.

PECS

My brother and I at a bar
in San Diego and luck
is all we ever talk about.

IPAs start to blur into lagoon water
bulrush and yerba
mansa, and we agree no portents

could have ever been thought up
for all of this.
The neon twenty-four-hour

signs. The sweet spot
in a Saturday night
where it opens up and wide like

someone saying *Dude you can
pay what's due
tomorrow.* We take control

of the juke box. Luck is all
we talk about.
Our country still down south,

both our parents sleeping
right up I-5.
At one a.m. the mirror

in the dark restroom
steadies. Focus.
Look how far you've come,

drunk with three cities
in your mouth,
Jalisco mustache

and a trucker's belly, sleeves cut
off to the love handles,
standing around like a new word

the whole coast got comfortable using.

NOVIEMBRE

I arrived here to day-old Halloween candy. In my aunt and uncle's living room,
unwrapping what would become a lifelong relationship with Almond Joy chocolate bars,
my uncle explained Halloween to me: pillowcases and polyester devil costumes.

At the foot of the bed they would sleep on in my cousin's old room, my father and
mother laid out some blankets for Lupita, Elias, and me.

My mother would not visit her mother's grave this year. She would help her family adjust
to Mission Viejo for eight days, Santa Ana and beyond for the rest of her life.
It's for the best. This is a new life. Memories of my grandmother.
This is a new life for your children, Lupe.

Lupe. So my kids won't have to work in the sun, in the fields, Lupe.
So my kids can work in an office with air conditioning, Lupe.
My hardworking father would buy me a Mr. T coloring book at Alpha Beta,
because he knew I was an artist.

We will find success here. We will fit in here. Pillowcases and polyester devil costumes.

COMPROMISO

Sharon knows the word
for excuse me: compromiso.
Imagines a waiter between
tables at a seafood restaurant in
Baja to remember it.
You know, a little faggot.
Compromiso!

Her pantomime of a pursed
lip and a swish strikes
my face, and I've never
been more grateful
for my mother's Spanish-
only ears.

My mother cooks for her and for her
husband the county inspector.
If the food and tequila stop,
the work may stop too. My father
reminds us often.

I sit with them beneath
the avocado tree
(which in its time will also contribute)
mostly quiet

knowing   it's two words:
con permiso—that un compromiso
means a commitment, an obligation—

knowing that Sharon wouldn't
stand for the little faggot at the
restaurant correcting her, that I
shouldn't do it either.

I'M AWARE I'LL GROW OLD

like my mother's father
and her brothers—proud
ruddy men of the plains,
copper brown hair ceding
to white in tight-lipped
lines.

Not without a fight.

The way my mother
defended what was theirs—
their property—while
my father worked
up north. Her holy spirit
fire.

Those parcels of ritual anger

I feel steaming in me too.
Honor of the landowner.
Sufficiency of cattle rancher.
Bronze-buttoned charro
of the high plain
with a magical control of twirling
lassos.

Even with all that in the mirror,

Father, when you died I
only wished for your humble hands
in fields of lettuce, your raw
fingers in steel beams, broad
arm bracing a machine to cut
into the growing fennel.

That navigating brown
core steering heart
pushing blood, moving
limb. Lungs in melody
still whistling of good
will and of fair labor.

SANTA ANA: DOWNTOWN

Sometimes the cold evenings
after work are filled with parrots.
No one knows how they got here,
how a couple of feathers fanned
out into this squawking-green sky
netting. *Where do they sleep?*

A white woman writes in an article,
her surprise in finding them
in the city. She admits her family knew
there would be changes when they
moved, but screaming parrots? She
calls this place her hood, she takes

the hood's good with the bad:
the Mexican food, the rest of the
unpalatable characteristics. Writes
about its history. All architecture.
Wonders if she'd been better off

with a Spanish-style home. It's not too late.
History. I think about how the Black
woman who lives across the street
from the house where I grew up had
to fight in court to lease an apartment
where she and her sweet husband could

sleep. History. Gardeners in front of
glowing donut shops before the sun
comes up. The neon signs, the tired
jokes on the AM radio. The laughter
of men who could make even coffee
bloom. Saving to buy a home of their

own. Renting garages and tiny rooms
in the meantime. Their children carving
out land for themselves, quiet places for

homework, where they can shyly radiate
with new words, long division and dreams.
Still, the new investors make promises

to bring the shine back. Exorcise the
downtown scrap yards—you, tell me
whether you are of this world or the
next, and I'll tell you where to eat.
The streamlined storefronts, cold
windows radiating the cleansing

frost. I once heard a man at the
barbershop give his reasons for
splitting a small stretch of Fourth
Street into an east and a west, in this
place where ten years ago cardinal
directions would have squealed out

of his head in a wrong-turn panic.
But where the hell do these parrots
come from, man? Damn invasion.
Oh, that house we just got is going
down next week, tearing the yard
out too, but we're definitely eating

the tangerines. And at the edges, I
can see the chayote vines reduced to
border filigree, swinging their spiny
pendulums below the living, floating,
breathing down, the mystifying cover
that is questioned then dispersed.

OTAY CROSSING

We are discharged from a womb,
its lining made of twenty lanes

    We are born

Again and again

    We have the letter to show and relive it

Our birth

And each time, the god at the booth presents us,
his hairy arm rising and straining its blue polyester:

        Born from nothing!
           Magic!
         Fully formed!

CLAPBOARD

In second grade I winged definitions
because I couldn't find a dictionary
among the hand-me-downs people
left in the house we moved into.

I described a wallet best I could:
the loose crease, the torn
corners. Fruit only shapes
and colors absent continents

of origin. The house on Spruce
with its two rooms for seven
people never promised more
than what it first contained,

but taught us to create space—
knees on the green carpet
with a notebook split open
on the edge of a mattress,

prayer and sewing taken up
at the kitchen table. Rough
shingles, drumming rain
gutters. In a way a house

never stops protecting us.
I can still see its lamp
shorting out, and my family
walking in the dark, feeling

our way around. Doing pretty well.

ALISO CREEK REST STOP, I-5-SB

We get a good honest view of California here. Everything it is: dry shift dress of a palm tree, concrete and a metal railing, tourist sign and the spin on the paths the friars plowed up the coast. The things we leave forever on its concrete benches, under the eucalyptus of its way stations. Cars and bodies once full and warm and comfortable. Stretches of fathers walking toward their children, seeing them now as they always have, disillusioned and remarkable. Here is summer in a state that can't see the full mass of its own body. Here is the talk of home, food, and future that's used to tie its hills to sheaf.

FORMAS FINALES

The steam train headed west from Atotonilco
had departed long ago. The one my father
sometimes jumped on as it slowed on a hill. Tired

child. The path lacking modern guides,
lacking guardrail and colonial arch. Electricity
was holy. Was softer. Was circuits of moonlight.
And the mothers' gold-embroidered hemlines

hovered closer when coyote rustled in the brush,
when rock loosened on the hillside. He prayed
to Our Holy Mother of San Juan de los Lagos.
Her crown with angels spinning like weather

vanes, the knives that ended her mortal life long
ago melted into a hydraulic crescent at her feet.
All over, stars counted down toward the dawn.
And a soft voice said I will try to protect you

as long as I can. Let me hold your hand, Juan.
If only while you and your children and theirs
begin to learn the sky's machinery.

WINTER CUMBIA WITH BROTHER AND SISTER
for Elias and Adanari

Drinking in different cities, all three of us
end up in restaurants where the air is synthesized
lavender and a steady bass line anchoring a sedge
of crane calls mimicked by a keyboard.
With our red eyes perched
on neon, elbows on yellow plastic tabletops,
we watch the night break apart in drafts
and coats through automatic doors. Weeks
have passed since we last saw each other,
and maybe this soft splintering is what comes
after grief allows us some form
of breath. But out here on my own, I
can still see the ways in which we try
to remind and connect ourselves with memory.
Tonight, it's by sharing the names of the songs
playing on the too-loud speakers bolted to the white
tile of these places, the times an accordion
unexpectedly completes a phrase and calls out
like a father in a sundown of reeds.

THE HEREAFTER

is, like everything around me,
built by my father. His feet in wood
frames full of mud and straw,
comically slowed down
by that strange small dog who ran ahead
to be his companion. Of course
there are bean sprouts growing
below the corn stalks, fields of wild
tuberose and the boulder ledges
of our river. The night filled
with oil lamp bright, noon songs
incomplete without some light
radio static. It will always be Jalisco.
I will just go out and say it. Say
that the eyes of those who are mine
adjust not to an ascent
as much as a return. After all
of our years, we finally set out
toward the right horizon.

ABOUT THE AUTHOR

Gustavo Hernandez is the author of the micro-chapbook *Form His Arms* (Ghost City Press). His work has previously been published in *Reed Magazine, The Acentos Review, Sonora Review* and other publications. He was born in Jalisco, Mexico and lives in Southern California. *Flower Grand First* is his first full-length collection of poems.

ACKNOWLEDGEMENTS

"Turquoise," "Third Shift," and "Noviembre" originally published in *Assaracus: A Journal of Gay Poetry* (2016)

"Along the 15 Near Baker" originally published in *Word Riot* (2016)

"I'm Aware I'll Grow Old" and "Refugio" originally published in *RipRap* (2018, 2019)

"Santa Ana, Fourth Grade" originally published in *Reed Magazine* (2018)

"Santa Ana: Downtown" and "Sunday, San Gabriel Valley" originally published in *Impossible Archetype* (2018)

"Baudelia" originally published in *The Acentos Review* (2018)

"Formas Sagradas" originally published in *Sonora Review* (2018) and anthologized in *Mother Mary Comes to Me: A Pop Culture Poetry Anthology* (2020)

"Winter Cumbia with Brother and Sister" originally published in *The Night Heron Barks* (2020)

"Clapboard" originally published in *Rattle's Poets Respond* (2020)

"Carmen" originally published in *The Los Angeles Review* (2020)

"1990/20XX" originally published in *Carve* (2021)

THIS BOOK IS ALSO DEDICATED TO
THOSE WHO HAVE RETURNED TO THE
HOMELAND AND WAIT FOR US THERE

Carmen y José Hurtado

Refugio Zarate

Camilo Hernandez

Rosario y Juan Lambaren

Juan "Vale" Hurtado

Baudelia Hurtado

Jesús, Domingo, y Manuel Hurtado

José Luis Zarate

Juan "Lolo" Hurtado

&

Fol

THANK YOU

~

Carmen, hermana, gracias por todo lo que hiciste y sigues haciendo por mi y por nuestra familia. Te quiero mucho.

Lupita, my guardian, the joy and support you bring to my life continue to change me for the better.

Salvador Elias, we have always been companions. This RPG would have been a lot more difficult without you by my side.

Adanari, my brilliant little sparkler, I love you. This book would not have been the same without your presence in it.

Magda + Liz + Kika + Cassie + Yuzu. The future is looking bright and all kinds of crazy.

Sergio, Ignacio, Satoko, and Miguel. My love and respect to all of you.

Richard. Thank you for your love and for your (saintly) patience.

~

Collin Kelley. I am so grateful for your advice and encouragement. It changed everything.

Eric Morago and Moon Tide. Thanks for believing in me and in this book.

Alexandra Umlas. You were the matchmaker. You are a terrific poet and a wonderful person. I'm lucky to know you.

Sarah Rafael García. Thank you for helping me to see our city again.

Steven Sanchez. Thank you for always supporting me. You are an inspiration.

Ángel García. Sharing a stage with you gave me the confidence and drive to keep working.

Bryan Borland and Seth Pennington. Thank you for helping this book find its true form.

Trevor Ketner, V. Ruiz, Tori Cardenas. You did so much for me and for this book. I am thankful to have worked with you all.

YOUR WORDS ARE REASONS WHY THIS BOOK EXISTS

Kelsey Gutierrez. Lynnette Beers. Will Lennertz. Marilynn Montaño. Jesús Cortez. Mark Ward. Christian Gullette. Megan Dorame. Michelle Brittan Rosado. Alan Chazaro. Kim Sousa. Michael Torres. Rogan Kelly and the Night Heron crew. Charles Harper Webb. Patty Seyburn. Omar Sakr. Angela Narciso Torres. Carl Phillips. Luke Johnson. Lane Berger. Chris Campanioni. Jessi Galanter. Stacy Russo. Randi Romo. Dare Williams. Charles Jensen. Lisa Alvarez. Robert Siek. Bryan Moats. Kai Coggin. Daniel Edward Moore. Vincent Cooper. Raymond Luczak. Edward Vidaurre. Anatalia Vallez. Sonia Gutiérrez. Lauren Camp. Darren C. Demaree. Stuart Barnes. Fred Schmalz. Robert Carr. Gris Muñoz. Ada Limón. Blas Falconer. Jason B. Crawford. Kevin Bertolero. Chris L. Butler. Ben Kline. Denzel Scott. Rachel McKibbens. Ines Pujos. Esteban Rodriguez. Dustin Brookshire. Steven Reigns. Isabel Quintero. Julie E. Bloemeke. Nancy Lynée Woo. Cynthia Atkins. Tiana Clark. Ruben Quesada.

HEARTFELT GRATITUDE IN A VARIETY OF FORMS

Duane and Antonio. Rudy García. Danielle, Fidel, Luke and Alex Ibarra. David and Julian. Ricky Rodriguez. William Claster. Barbara Allen. Jamoa Moberly. Isabel Bañuelos. Manuel Galaviz. Carla Zarate Suarez. Sali Heraldez. Bethanie Qoe. Travis Orme. The Hernandez and Sanchez families. Tara and Raúl.

TO MY ENTIRE COMMUNITY OF FAMILY AND FRIENDS: THANK YOU FOR BEING HERE WITH ME

NOTES

FORMAS SAGRADAS

Big thank you to my brother, Elias, for guiding me to these figures in the Jalisco sky.

BLAS

My father said the orange tabby was never given a name. Somewhere in my files there is an unfinished draft of a story where his name is Blas.

SANTA ANA: DOWNTOWN

This poem was written in one go after I first read Tiana Clark's "Nashville." The line "Tell me whether you are of this world or the next" comes from *The Lean Lands* by Agustín Yañez.

TUBEROSE

The tuberose facts and etymological history in this poem come from the article "'Omixochitl' the Tuberose (Polianthes tuberosa)" by Emily W. Emmart Trueblood (1973)

ALSO AVAILABLE FROM MOON TIDE PRESS

Everything is Radiant Between the Hates, Rich Ferguson (2020)
When the Pain Starts: Poetry as Sequential Art, Alan Passman (2020)
This Place Could Be Haunted If I Didn't Believe in Love, Lincoln McElwee (2020)
Impossible Thirst, Kathryn de Lancellotti (2020)
Lullabies for End Times, Jennifer Bradpiece (2020)
Crabgrass World, Robin Axworthy (2020)
Contortionist Tongue, Dania Ayah Alkhouli (2020)
The only thing that makes sense is to grow, Scott Ferry (2020)
Dead Letter Box, Terri Niccum (2019)
Tea and Subtitles: Selected Poems 1999-2019, Michael Miller (2019)
At the Table of the Unknown, Alexandra Umlas (2019)
The Book of Rabbits, Vince Trimboli (2019)
Everything I Write Is a Love Song to the World, David McIntire (2019)
Letters to the Leader, HanaLena Fennel (2019)
Darwin's Garden, Lee Rossi (2019)
Dark Ink: A Poetry Anthology Inspired by Horror (2018)
Drop and Dazzle, Peggy Dobreer (2018)
Junkie Wife, Alexis Rhone Fancher (2018)
The Moon, My Lover, My Mother, & the Dog, Daniel McGinn (2018)
Lullaby of Teeth: An Anthology of Southern California Poetry (2017)
Angels in Seven, Michael Miller (2016)
A Likely Story, Robbi Nester (2014)
Embers on the Stairs, Ruth Bavetta (2014)
The Green of Sunset, John Brantingham (2013)
The Savagery of Bone, Timothy Matthew Perez (2013)
The Silence of Doorways, Sharon Venezio (2013)
Cosmos: An Anthology of Southern California Poetry (2012)
Straws and Shadows, Irena Praitis (2012)
In the Lake of Your Bones, Peggy Dobreer (2012)
I Was Building Up to Something, Susan Davis (2011)
Hopeless Cases, Michael Kramer (2011)
One World, Gail Newman (2011)
What We Ache For, Eric Morago (2010)
Now and Then, Lee Mallory (2009)
Pop Art: An Anthology of Southern California Poetry (2009)
In the Heaven of Never Before, Carine Topal (2008)
A Wild Region, Kate Buckley (2008)

Carving in Bone: An Anthology of Orange County Poetry (2007)
Kindness from a Dark God, Ben Trigg (2007)
A Thin Strand of Lights, Ricki Mandeville (2006)
Sleepyhead Assassins, Mindy Nettifee (2006)
Tide Pools: An Anthology of Orange County Poetry (2006)
Lost American Nights: Lyrics & Poems, Michael Ubaldini (2006)

PATRONS

Moon Tide Press would like to thank the following people for their support in helping publish the finest poetry from the Southern California region. To sign up as a patron, visit www.moontidepress.com or send an email to publisher@moontidepress.com.

Anonymous
Robin Axworthy
Conner Brenner
Bill Cushing
Susan Davis
Peggy Dobreer
Dennis Gowans
Alexis Rhone Fancher
HanaLena Fennel
Half Off Books & Brad T. Cox
Donna Hilbert
Jim & Vicky Hoggatt
Michael Kramer
Ron Koertge & Bianca Richards
Ray & Christi Lacoste
Zachary & Tammy Locklin
Lincoln McElwee
David McIntire
José Enrique Medina
Michael Miller & Rachanee Srisavasdi
Michelle & Robert Miller
Ronny & Richard Morago
Terri Niccum
Andrew November
Jennifer Smith
Andrew Turner
Rex Wilder
Mariano Zaro

in light and dew and smoke

all the young stalks of the earth

lift the summer dust

chaining the clovered horizon to garland

primary colors warming

public pilgrimages

electric arrows

say you still hear our parents calling

crescent, bullhorn, new to full

electric arrows

glint of a finch song in the nochebuena

finite iridescence

electric arrows

ruche of meadow gathered along the river

our fathers in the sky

FLOWER GRAND FIRST

Made in USA - Kendallville, IN
1231754_9781735037837
02.11.2021 0837